T0380962

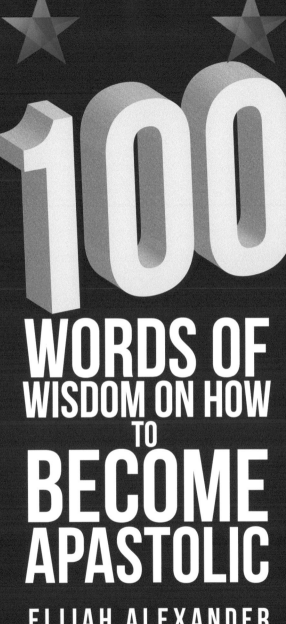

# 100

# WORDS OF
## WISDOM ON HOW
### TO
# BECOME
# APASTOLIC

## ELIJAH ALEXANDER

To order additional copies of this book, contact:
Xlibris
1-888-795-4274
www.Xlibris.com
Orders@Xlibris.com

# 100

## WORDS OF
### WISDOM ON HOW
### TO
## BECOME
## APASTOLIC

1. For the Lord of Host's would speak unto thee Dancing
   in the spirit is true if you do it for the Lord.

2. For the Lord of Host's would speak unto thee
   Dancing is good as long as there's no sin in it.

3. For the Lord of Host's would speak unto
   thee Dancing is good exercise.

4. For the Lord of Host's would speak unto thee
   Dancing delivers and can set you free.

5. For the Lord of Host's would speak unto
   thee do not be ashamed of Dancing.

6. For the Lord of Host's would speak unto thee Dance but do it correctly.

7. For the Lord of Host's would speak unto thee Lift up Holy hands.

8. For the Lord of Host's would speak unto thee Go by thee entire Bible.

9. For the Lord of Host's would speak unto thee let the Bible change thee.

10. For the Lord of Host's would speak unto thee Laughing in the spirit is Apastolic.

11.  For the Lord of Host's would speak unto thee
accept life the way it supposed to be.

12.  For the Lord of Host's would speak unto
thee if thou art Apastolic change not.

13.  For the Lord of Host's would speak unto thee
overcoming evil with good can be Apastolic.

14.  For the Lord of Host's would speak unto thee
getting out of Sin can be Apastolic.

15.  For the Lord of Host's would speak unto thee
Being Apastolic and changing not is Apastolic.

16. For the Lord of Host's would speak unto
    thee being kind can be Apastolic.

17. For the Lord of Host's would speak unto thee
    that there's nothing Apastolic in pride.

18. For the Lord of Host's would speak unto
    thee Being generous can be apastolic.

19. For the Lord of Host's would speak unto thee It's
    Gods will that all churches be Apastolic.

20. For the Lord of Host's would speak unto
    thee a merry Heart can be Apastolic.

21. For the Lord of Host's would speak unto thee If your church is not Apastolic it will dry up and become dead.

22. For the Lord of Host's would speak unto thee If you are Apastolic you will overcome.

23. For the Lord of Host's would speak unto thee Be Apastolic It's Gods will.

24. For the Lord of Host's would speak unto thee sharing can be Apastolic.

25. For the Lord of Host's would speak unto thee Apastolic will deliver from sin.

26. For the Lord of Host's would speak unto
thee I am the law giver, be Apastolic.

27. For the Lord of Host's would speak unto thee
that there's deliverance in being Apastolic.

28. For the Lord of Host's would speak
unto thee Apastolic is life.

29. For the Lord of Host's would speak unto thee David
danced with all his might that's being Apastolic.

30. For the Lord of Host's would speak unto thee
Anointing thyself with oil can be Apastolic.

31. For the Lord of Host's would speak unto
thee Being anointed is Apastolic.

32. For the Lord of Host's would speak unto thee
Being unashamed is being Apastolic.

33. For the Lord of Host's would speak unto thee
Dancing for joy is being Apastolic.

34. For the Lord of Host's would speak unto
thee Giving can be Apastolic.

35. For the Lord of Host's would speak unto
thee if your Apastolic change not.

36. For the Lord of Host's would speak unto thee obeying the 10 commandments can be Apastolic.

37. For the Lord of Host's would speak unto thee there's Apastolicness in being caring.

38. For the Lord of Host's would speak unto thee Being humorous can be Apastolic.

39. For the Lord of Host's would speak unto thee Dancing in righteousness is good.

40. For the Lord of Host's would speak unto thee Follow after righteousness and you will be Apastolic.

41. For the Lord of Host's would speak unto thee
If Jesus was Apastolic why shouldn't we?

42. For the Lord of Host's would speak unto thee If you don't
know how to be Apastolic ask someone to show you how.

43. For the Lord of Host's would speak unto thee If
you go by the Bible you will be Apastolic.

44. For the Lord of Host's would speak unto thee
If you're not Apastolic become Apastolic.

45. For the Lord of Host's would speak unto thee
Being Apastolic is a good way to live.

46. For the Lord of Host's would speak unto thee Do your best to become Apastolic and you will be.

47. For the Lord of Host's would speak unto thee Do not resist being Apastolic.

48. For the Lord of Host's would speak unto thee The world desparately needs to be Apastolic.

49. For the Lord of Host's would speak unto thee Judge for yourself, be honest about being Apastolic if you do you will know it is correct.

50. For the Lord of Host's would speak unto thee God wants us to be Apastolic.

51. For the Lord of Host's would speak unto thee To be Apastolic will deliver you from problems.

52. For the Lord of Host's would speak unto thee If you become Apastolic you will overcome.

53. For the Lord of Host's would speak unto thee Being Apastolic will?

54. For the Lord of Host's would speak unto thee Our churches are in desperate need to become Apastolic.

55. For the Lord of Host's would speak unto thee Be Apastolic and watch problems vanish away.

56. For the Lord of Host's would speak unto thee Why not become Apastolic now it will save you a lot of problems.

57. For the Lord of Host's would speak unto thee cheer up if your Apastolic because you going thee correct way.

58. For the Lord of Host's would speak unto thee If you're being Apastolic you are being Apastolic and that is good.

59. For the Lord of Host's would speak unto thee Being Apastolic is a way to overcome.

60. For the Lord of Host's would speak unto thee Being Apastolic is a great way to live.

61. For the Lord of Host's would speak unto thee Being Apastolic is joy. So why not be Apastolic.

62. For the Lord of Host's would speak unto thee Being Apastolic is nothing to be ashamed of.

63. For the Lord of Host's would speak unto thee Being Apastolic is correct if you are right.

64. For the Lord of Host's would speak unto thee Being Apastolic helps the burden to be light.

65. For the Lord of Host's would speak unto thee Being Apastolic is good.

66. For the Lord of Host's would speak unto thee
Please become Apastolic if you aren't.

67. For the Lord of Host's would speak unto
thee Being Apastolic overcomes and as you're
in it you will remain overcoming.

68. For the Lord of Host's would speak unto
thee Joy comes from being Apastolic.

69. For the Lord of Host's would speak unto
thee Being friendly can be Apastolic.

70. For the Lord of Host's would speak unto thee
You will overcome if your Apastolic and you
will grow dead if you're not Apastolic.

71. For the Lord of Host's would speak unto
thee Apastolic is righteousness.

72. For the Lord of Host's would speak unto thee
Great is your joy if you are Apastolic/

73. For the Lord of Host's would speak unto thee
Everyone that's Apastolic overcometh.

74. For the Lord of Host's would speak unto thee
If you're not Apastolic you're missing out.

75. For the Lord of Host's would speak unto thee
If you're Apastolic you will be Happy.

76. For the Lord of Host's would speak
unto thee Jesus is Apastolic.

77. For the Lord of Host's would speak unto thee If you're not
Apastolic and you become Apastolic it's a new way to live.

78. For the Lord of Host's would speak unto thee Joy,
peace and laughter come from being Apastolic.

79. For the Lord of Host's would speak unto
thee If you're not Apastolic, Pray thru.

80. For the Lord of Host's would speak unto thee
Angels are present when you're Apastolic.

81. For the Lord of Host's would speak unto thee
    You're in a danger zone if you're not Apastolic.

82. For the Lord of Host's would speak unto thee
    God bless's you when you're Apastolic.

83. For the Lord of Host's would speak unto thee If Apastolic
    is right it is right so why not become Apastolic.

84. For the Lord of Host's would speak unto thee If you're
    Apastolic your life is changed as if you weren't.

85. For the Lord of Host's would speak unto thee if
    you know being Apastolic is right, do it.

86. For the Lord of Host's would speak unto thee
God rejoices when your Apastolic.

87. For the Lord of Host's would speak unto thee
You are a changed person if you're Apastolic
if not you would dry up spiritually.

88. For the Lord of Host's would speak unto
thee right is right and being Apastolic is right
and there's nothing wrong about it.

89. For the Lord of Host's would speak unto thee
Becoming Apastolic means your overcoming.

90. For the Lord of Host's would speak unto
thee change not if you're Apastolic.

91. For the Lord of Host's would speak unto thee Apastolic people Help people become Apastolic who aren't.

92. For the Lord of Host's would speak unto thee Being Apastolic means you have the victory.

93. For the Lord of Host's would speak unto thee If you're not Apastolic become Apastolic it's a new way to live.

94. For the Lord of Host's would speak unto thee Being Apastolic comes from God.

95. For the Lord of Host's would speak unto thee Being Apastolic is full of good things.

96.  For the Lord of Host's would speak unto thee Being
Apastolic is the way everyone should live.

97.  For the Lord of Host's would speak unto thee
you cannot fail if you're Apastolic.

98.  For the Lord of Host's would speak unto thee You're
not a failure if you're Apastolic but you are saved.

99.  For the Lord of Host's would speak unto
thee All is well if you're Apastolic.

100.  For the Lord of Host's would speak unto thee Be
Apastolic. Be free. Be saved. Be Happy and overcome.

Printed in the United States
By Bookmasters